Contents

P9-BJC-721

To the Reader

There are eight stories in this book. They come from around the world. I picked these stories because I like them very much. I think that you will like them too.

The stories are fun to read. The exercises will be fun to do too. They will help you read and write better. You will also find out about the parts of a story such as the *plot*.

First go over the words in **Before You Read.** Make sure you know what each word means. This will help when you read the story.

Later, do the exercises after each of the stories. See how well you do on these TESTS:

TELL ABOUT THE STORY.

END EACH LINE.

SHOW WHAT WORDS MEAN.

THINK ABOUT THE STORY.

SPOT PARTS OF A STORY.

TELL ABOUT THE STORY helps you find things that happened in the story. These are sometimes called *facts*.

END EACH LINE helps you with your reading and vocabulary (what words mean). This part uses fill-in, or cloze, exercises.

SHOW WHAT WORDS MEAN helps you build your vocabulary. The vocabulary words in each story are in **dark letters.** You may look back at these words when you do the vocabulary questions.

THINK ABOUT THE STORY asks *critical thinking* questions. This means you will have to think about what happened in the story. Then you will have to work out the answers.

SPOT PARTS OF A STORY goes over *character, plot,* and *setting.* On page 3 you will find the meanings of these words. You may look back at the meanings when you do the questions.

There is one other part. It is called THINK SOME MORE ABOUT THE STORY. This part helps you to think, talk, and *write* about the story.

There are four questions for each of the TESTS exercises. Here is the way to do the exercises:

- Do all the exercises.

- Go over your answers with your teacher.

- At the end of each exercise, write in your score for that exercise. Each question is worth 5 points. There are four questions, so you can get up to 20 points.

- You will find a TESTS chart after all of the exercises. Use this chart to add up your TOTAL SCORE. If you get all the questions right, your score will be 100.

- Keep track of how well you do. First write your TOTAL SCORE on the **Progress Chart** on page 120. Then write your score on the **Progress Graph** on page 121. Look at the **Progress Graph** to see how much your scores go up.

I know you will like the stories in this book. And the exercises will help you read and write better.

Now . . . get ready for *More Travels.*

Burton Goodman

The Short Story—
Character, Plot, and Setting

Character: someone in a story. You can tell what the *character* is like by what the character says and does. The way a character looks may also be important.

Plot: what happens in a story. The first thing that happens in a story is the first thing in the *plot*. The last thing that happens in a story is the last thing in the plot.

Setting: where and when the story takes place. The *setting* is the time and place of the story.

1
Answer Me This

a story from Spain

Before You Read

Before you read "Answer Me This," go over the words below. Make sure you know what each word means. This will help you when you read the story.

mayor: someone who is the head of a village, city, or town. The *mayor* helped the people of the village.

jacket: a short coat. Pablo was wearing a white *jacket*.

scarf: something that you wear around your head or your neck. You can put on a *scarf* to keep warm.

rode: was carried along. The king *rode* on a horse.

Answer Me This

a story from Spain

Τhis happened long ago. It happened in Spain.

The people gave money to the king. But the king was **greedy.** He said, "I do not have enough money. I will ride around the country. I will try to get more money."

One day the king came to a village. It was called Rios. The people of Rios were poor. They did not have much money.

The king did not care. He went to the village hall.

The king stopped a woman. The king said, "Tell me. Who is the mayor?"

The woman said, "Pablo is the mayor. He always wears a white jacket. Look. There he is now."

The king went up to Pablo. He said, "I am the king. The people of Rios must give me more money."

Pablo was surprised. "More money?" he said. "But the people here are poor. They have to buy food. They have to buy clothes. They give money to you now. They do not have much money."

There was a box in the village hall.

"What is that?" said the king.

He pointed to the box. It was made out of wood. There was a hole in the top. There were words on the box. The words said *FOR FOOD.*

Pablo answered. "It is just as I said. The people here are poor. Some have no money for food. But their neighbors are kind. Now and then they find a few cents. They put them in the box. We use that money to buy food. We give the food to the people."

The king said to himself, "These people are not poor. They give money away! They should give *me* that money! I will put a new mayor here. *My* mayor will get me more money!"

So the king said, "Pablo. A mayor must be **smart.** Are you smart? I will see. I will come back tomorrow morning. I will ask you three questions. You must tell me the answers. If your answers are right, you can still be the mayor. If your answers are not right, I will find a new mayor."

The king laughed to himself. Then he left the village hall.

Pablo wondered what to do. He called the people together. He told them what happened.

They said, "The king wants a new mayor. We do not want a new mayor. What can we do?"

There was a baker in Rios. The baker's name was Roberto. Roberto was smart. He was very, very smart. He was smarter than anyone in the village.

Someone said, "See if Roberto can help us. Go to his house. Tell him what happened. Hear what he says."

Pablo went to Roberto. He told Roberto the story.

Roberto thought for a long time. Then Roberto said, "Pablo, I will take your place tomorrow. I will try to answer the three questions."

Pablo looked worried.

Roberto said, "Do not worry. The king will not know it is me. Give me your white jacket."

Pablo took off his jacket. He gave it to Roberto.

Roberto said, "Now go to the village hall. Make sure there is no fire in the fireplace. There must be no **heat** in the hall. It must be very cold."

Morning came. Roberto got up very early. He put on Pablo's white jacket. Then he put on a big hat. The hat came down to his ears. Roberto found a long scarf. He threw it around himself. With the hat and the scarf, you could not see Roberto's face.

Roberto went to the village hall. He waited for the king. Soon the king came riding up. He came with his men. There were some villagers with them.

"Good morning, King," said Roberto.

"Good morning," said the king. "It is cold in this hall."

"Yes," Roberto said. "We will make a fire later. That way we do not use so much wood. We will **save** money. But I wear this hat and this scarf. They keep me warm."

"I see," said the king. "Now, are you ready for my questions?"

"I am ready," said Roberto.

"Well then," said the king. "Answer me this. How far can a dog run into the woods?"

Roberto thought. Then he said, "A dog can run to the middle of the woods. After that it runs out of the woods."

"A good answer," said the king. "But that was not hard. I will ask you the second question. Answer me this. What is the way to stop fish from smelling?"

Roberto said, "That is easy. Cut off their noses."

"A good answer," said the king. "A very good answer. But now I will ask you a question you will not be able to answer. Answer me this. What am I thinking?"

Roberto smiled. "Oh," he said. "That is the easiest question of all! You are thinking that I am Pablo the mayor. But I am really Roberto the baker!"

Roberto pulled off his hat. He pulled off his scarf. The king saw it was so.

The villagers started to laugh. Even the king had to laugh. The king's men began to laugh. They all stood there laughing.

Then the king told the villagers, "Pablo can still be your mayor."

The king went out the door. The king's men went with him. They got on their horses. They rode away from Rios. They never came back. Pablo stayed there as the mayor. And the king did not get the money he came for.

TELL ABOUT THE STORY.

Put an X in the box next to the right answer. Each answer tells something (a *fact*) about the story.

1. The king came to Rios to get
   - ☐ a. food.
   - ☐ b. water.
   - ☐ c. money.

2. Pablo said that the people of Rios were
   - ☐ a. happy.
   - ☐ b. poor.
   - ☐ c. very sad.

3. Roberto asked Pablo to give him his
   - ☐ a. hat.
   - ☐ b. horse.
   - ☐ c. jacket.

4. At the end of the story, the king began to
   - ☐ a. laugh.
   - ☐ b. cry.
   - ☐ c. jump up and down.

END EACH LINE.

Finish the lines below. Fill in each empty space with one of the words in the box. Each word can be found in the story. There are five words and four empty spaces. This means that one word in the box will not be used. The first word has been done for you.

See if you are able to answer this

<u>question</u>. "What kinds of animals
<small>1</small>

can jump higher _____ a
<small>2</small>

house?"

The _____ is "All kinds of
<small>3</small>

animals." That is because

_____ cannot jump.
<small>4</small>

answer		question
	want	
houses		than

NUMBER CORRECT X 5 = YOUR SCORE

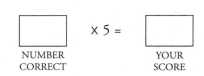

NUMBER CORRECT X 5 = YOUR SCORE

SHOW WHAT WORDS MEAN.

The words below are printed in **dark letters** in the story. You may look back at these vocabulary words before you answer the questions. Put an X in the box next to the right answer.

1. The greedy king wanted more money. The word *greedy* means
    - ☐ a. to want a lot.
    - ☐ b. to want very little.
    - ☐ c. to want nothing at all.

2. He wanted to see if Pablo was smart. Someone who is *smart* must
    - ☐ a. be very strong.
    - ☐ b. be very old.
    - ☐ c. know many things.

3. There was no heat in the hall. The word *heat* means
    - ☐ a. wet.
    - ☐ b. cold.
    - ☐ c. warm or hot.

4. The people tried to save money. The word *save* means to
    - ☐ a. give something away.
    - ☐ b. keep something for later.
    - ☐ c. look everywhere.

THINK ABOUT THE STORY.

Here is how to answer these questions. First think about what happened in the story. Then work out the right answers. This is called *critical thinking*.

1. The king thought Roberto was the mayor because
    - ☐ a. the king did not know what the mayor looked like.
    - ☐ b. the king could not see Roberto's face.
    - ☐ c. everyone said that Roberto was the mayor.

2. The king thought Roberto was Pablo because Roberto was
    - ☐ a. wearing Pablo's hat.
    - ☐ a. wearing Pablo's scarf.
    - ☐ c. wearing Pablo's white jacket.

3. It is fair to say that Roberto
    - ☐ a. tricked the king.
    - ☐ b. was not a good baker.
    - ☐ c. could not think fast.

4. At the end of the story, the people must have felt
    - ☐ a. angry.
    - ☐ b. happy.
    - ☐ c. sad.

☐ X 5 = ☐	☐ X 5 = ☐
NUMBER CORRECT YOUR SCORE	NUMBER CORRECT YOUR SCORE

SPOT PARTS OF A STORY.

Stories have **characters**, a **plot**, and a **setting**. (See page 3.) Put an X in the box next to the right answer.

1. What happened first? (**Plot**)
   - ☐ a. Roberto pulled off his hat.
   - ☐ b. The king came to Rios.
   - ☐ c. Pablo went to Roberto's house.

2. Which best tells about Roberto? (**Character**)
   - ☐ a. He was very smart.
   - ☐ b. He was very young.
   - ☐ c. He had a lot of money.

3. Where does the story take place? (**Setting**)
   - ☐ a. in Spain
   - ☐ b. in France
   - ☐ c. in the United States

4. When does the story take place? (**Setting**)
   - ☐ a. a year ago
   - ☐ b. two years ago
   - ☐ c. a long time ago

THINK SOME MORE ABOUT THE STORY.

Your teacher might want you to write your answers.

- Roberto put on a big hat and a long scarf. Why?
- Why did Roberto wear Pablo's white jacket?
- Why did Roberto want it to be cold in the village hall?

Write your scores in the box below. Then write your scores on pages 120 and 121.

☐ +	**T**ELL ABOUT THE STORY
☐ +	**E**ND EACH LINE
☐ +	**S**HOW WHAT WORDS MEAN
☐ +	**T**HINK ABOUT THE STORY
☐ =	**S**POT PARTS OF A STORY
☐	TOTAL SCORE: **Story 1**

☐ × 5 = ☐

NUMBER CORRECT   YOUR SCORE

2
The Game

by Scott C. Mason, Jr.

Before You Read

Before you read "The Game," go over the words below. Make sure you know what each word means. This will help you when you read the story.

weekend: Saturday and Sunday. Most people do not go to work on the *weekend.*

safe: a strong, heavy box for holding money and other important things. Put the money in the *safe.*

dial: something that is round and has numbers on it. The man turned the *dial* to open the safe.

jewels: things such as rings and pins made of gold. She was wearing beautiful *jewels.*

The Game

by Scott C. Mason, Jr.

J ane Peters and I were never good friends. We knew each other in high school. We were in some classes together. But that was about it.

You see, we were very different. Jane was tall and beautiful. I was not. She was on the basketball **team.** I was not. She went out with a lot of boys. I did not.

Two months ago, I moved back to town. Last week I got a call from Jane. I was very surprised.

She said, "I heard you were back. I thought I would give you a call. Why don't you visit me some time? You can come for a weekend."

As I said, I was surprised. But most of my friends had moved away. I did not know many people. So I said yes.

Jane lived in a big house. It looked very nice. Jane met me at the front door. She was still very beautiful. I looked a little better now. But I did not look like Jane.

"Pam!" Jane said. "It has been five years! They went by so fast. It is great to see you again!"

I said, "It is great to see you, too." I did not really mean it. But I had to say something.

Jane showed me to my room. It was very big. It was bigger than the place I lived in. I put my things away. Jane said, "Pam, I will make dinner for us."

I did not cook very well. But Jane was a very good cook. She said it many times. I almost hoped that she would burn something. But she did not. Everything that Jane made was great.

At dinner Jane kept talking about our high school days. I wanted to talk about something else. High school was not the best time of my life. But Jane went on talking about herself.

They were great days for Jane. She got the best **marks** in her classes. She was the best player on the basketball team. She knew almost everyone in school. Yes, Jane had many happy times. And she talked about them all. Over and over. Again and again. There was nothing I could do. I just listened to her.

After dinner we went into the living room. We played cards and some games. Jane beat me each time.

Jane was getting ready to beat me again. Then I saw an old safe. It was in a corner of the room. Its black paint was coming off. It must have been there a long time.

I asked Jane about the safe.

She said, "It was here when I moved in. The people before me found it. It was down in the **cellar.** They said it was here when they moved in. They found it that way. They never opened it."

"They never opened it?" I said.

"That is right," said Jane. "They did not know what numbers would open the safe. They did not care about the safe. But I brought it up here."

"Why?" I asked.

"Oh, friends visit me. Then we sometimes play a little game. We take turns trying to open the safe. The one who can open it can keep anything that is inside. I mean, *if* there is anything inside. Do you want to play the game?"

For once I *did* want to play! This time I knew I could win! I had once worked in a place where they made safes. I knew a lot about safes!

I had listened to Jane's stories about how great high school was. I knew she had a big house. I knew she was a good cook. I had lost all the games we played. Now it was time for *me* to win!

Yes, I wanted to play! She did not know that I knew something about safes!

But I needed more time. "I am tired now," I said. "Let us wait until tomorrow."

I got into bed. I was tired. But I could not fall asleep. I kept thinking about the safe. I thought about turning the dial on the safe. I thought about opening the door. I thought about finding something great inside! Yes, I wanted to find something great. Something like jewels!

I thought about the look that would be on Jane's face when she saw the jewels. For once *I* would beat Jane at something! For once *she* would feel the way she made other people feel. I kept thinking about that. It made me happy.

We ate breakfast the next morning. Then Jane said, "Let us go outside."

There was a basketball hoop near the house. There was a basketball on the ground. Jane picked it up.

"Come on," Jane said. "Let us play a game. Let us shoot some baskets. The one who gets ten baskets first wins."

We played three times. Jane won every game. The games were not even close.

Jane could beat me at anything. That was how it seemed. Then I thought about the safe. Now *I* would have the last laugh!

After lunch we went into the living room. We walked over to the safe. I was very excited. But I tried not to show it.

"All right," said Jane. "You can go first."

I put my ear next to the dial. I turned the dial very slowly. I heard a sound. I had found one of the numbers!

My heart was beating wildly. Jane was watching me. She was smiling. I laughed to myself. Jane would *not* win this time!

I had brought some clothes to Jane's house. I also brought some other things. I brought some of my grandmother's old jewels. I knew they were **worth** money. So I always took them with me.

Last night I had waited until Jane was in bed. Then I went into the living room. I went there slowly. I did not make any noise. I had a lot of time. I was able to open the safe. I looked inside. The safe was empty. But I did not leave it that way! No! I put the jewels inside. Then I locked the door again.

Now I made believe it was hard to open the safe. I took my time. I turned the dial slowly to the left. I turned it slowly to the right.

Jane was smiling. Well, that smile would soon leave her face. She would not smile when I took out the jewels! Then *I* would be the winner! I would be the winner at last!

I turned the dial one more time. Then I stopped. I waited before I opened the door. This was going to be great! How surprised Jane would be. She would think that the jewels had been there all the time!

I pulled open the door of the safe. I looked in the safe. I was ready to say, "Jane! Just look at this!"

But I never said those words.

The safe was empty! But how could that be?

Then I knew. Jane had taken the jewels that I had put there.

I looked at Jane's face. Jane smiled at me. "Remember," she said. "The one who can open the safe can keep what is inside."

I had lost once again.

TELL ABOUT THE STORY.

Put an X in the box next to the right answer. Each answer tells something (a *fact*) about the story.

1. Pam said that she and Jane were
   - ☐ a. good friends.
   - ☐ b. very different.
   - ☐ c. tall and beautiful.

2. Jane and Pam had not seen each other for
   - ☐ a. about a year.
   - ☐ b. five years.
   - ☐ c. ten years.

3. At dinner, Jane kept talking about
   - ☐ a. herself.
   - ☐ b. the town.
   - ☐ c. Pam.

4. At night, Pam opened the safe and put in
   - ☐ a. a letter.
   - ☐ b. money.
   - ☐ c. jewels.

END EACH LINE.

Finish the lines below. Fill in each empty space with one of the words in the box. Each word can be found in the story. There are five words and four empty spaces. This means that one word in the box will not be used.

The first basketball _____
1

was played in 1891. At that time

there were nine _____ on each
2

side. The game has changed a lot over

the _____. Today there are
3

five players on _____ side.
4

years	school
game	
each	players

SHOW WHAT WORDS MEAN.

The words below are printed in **dark letters** in the story. You may look back at these vocabulary words before you answer the questions. Put an X in the box next to the right answer.

1. Jane was on the basketball team. As used here, *team* means people who
   - ☐ a. work in different places.
   - ☐ b. play together.
   - ☐ c. do not know each other.

2. Jane got good marks in school. What are *marks?*
   - ☐ a. the teachers you have
   - ☐ b. the friends in your class
   - ☐ c. numbers or letters that show how well you have done

3. They kept it down in the cellar. The *cellar* is the part of the house that is
   - ☐ a. below the ground.
   - ☐ b. on the roof.
   - ☐ c. in the living room.

4. Pam knew they were worth money. The word *worth* means
   - ☐ a. how big something is.
   - ☐ b. how old something is.
   - ☐ c. how much you can sell something for.

☐ X 5 =	☐
NUMBER CORRECT	YOUR SCORE

THINK ABOUT THE STORY.

Here is how to answer these questions. First think about what happened in the story. Then work out the right answers. This is called *critical thinking.*

1. Pam wanted to
   - ☐ a. be Jane's best friend.
   - ☐ b. beat Jane at something.
   - ☐ c. talk about her high school days.

2. We can guess that Jane thought Pam might
   - ☐ a. put something in the safe.
   - ☐ b. stay for a week.
   - ☐ c. win all the games they played.

3. Which one is true?
   - ☐ a. Pam could not open the safe.
   - ☐ b. Pam surprised Jane.
   - ☐ c. Jane opened the safe.

4. We can guess that Pam
   - ☐ a. did not visit Jane again.
   - ☐ b. visited Jane many more times.
   - ☐ c. got the jewels back from Jane.

☐ X 5 =	☐
NUMBER CORRECT	YOUR SCORE

SPOT PARTS OF A STORY.

Stories have **characters**, a **plot**, and a **setting**. (See page 3.) Put an X in the box next to the right answer.

1. What happened first? (**Plot**)
   - ☐ a. Pam opened the safe.
   - ☐ b. Pam went to Jane's house.
   - ☐ c. Pam ate dinner with Jane.

2. Which best tells about Pam? (**Character**)
   - ☐ a. She was a very good cook.
   - ☐ b. She played basketball very well.
   - ☐ c. She kept losing to Jane.

3. Where does the story take place? (**Setting**)
   - ☐ a. in a school
   - ☐ b. in a store
   - ☐ c. in a house in a town

4. When does the story take place? (**Setting**)
   - ☐ a. now
   - ☐ b. last year
   - ☐ c. long ago

THINK SOME MORE ABOUT THE STORY.

Your teacher might want you to write your answers.

- Why do you think Jane asked Pam to visit her?
- Did you like Jane? Why?
- At the end of the story, did you feel sorry for Pam? Why?

Write your scores in the box below. Then write your scores on pages 120 and 121.

☐ +	**T**ELL ABOUT THE STORY
☐ +	**E**ND EACH LINE
☐ +	**S**HOW WHAT WORDS MEAN
☐ +	**T**HINK ABOUT THE STORY
☐ =	**S**POT PARTS OF A STORY
☐	TOTAL SCORE: **Story 2**

☐ × 5 = ☐

NUMBER CORRECT   YOUR SCORE

31

3
The Champ

by Sulamith Ish-Kishor

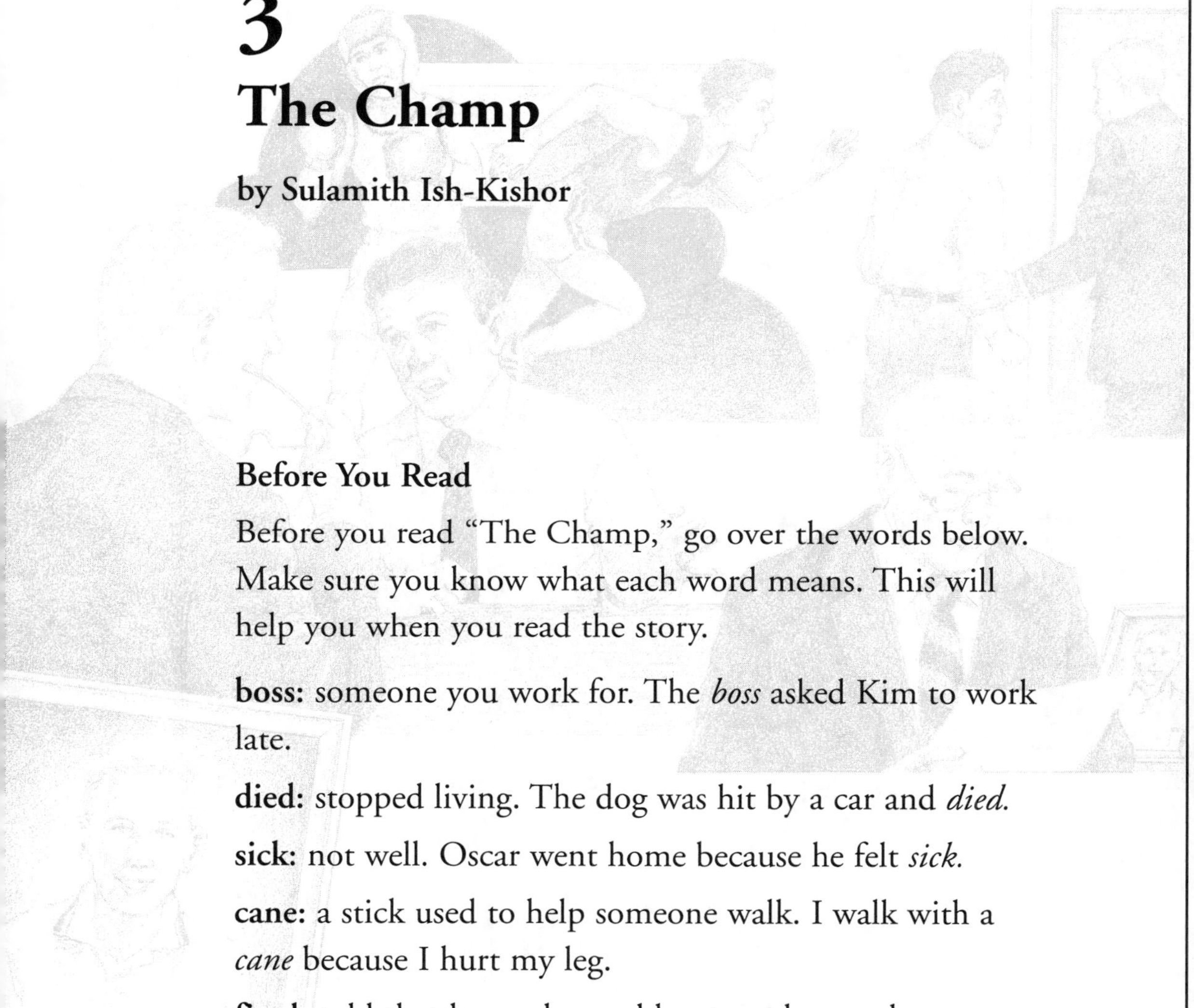

Before You Read

Before you read "The Champ," go over the words below.
Make sure you know what each word means. This will
help you when you read the story.

boss: someone you work for. The *boss* asked Kim to work
late.

died: stopped living. The dog was hit by a car and *died.*

sick: not well. Oscar went home because he felt *sick.*

cane: a stick used to help someone walk. I walk with a
cane because I hurt my leg.

fired: told that he or she could not work at a place
anymore. When you are *fired,* you lose your job.

boxer: someone who fights someone else in a sport. The
boxer fights once a week.

champion: someone who wins or comes in first. The
champion runner won every race.

The Champ

by Sulamith Ish-Kishor

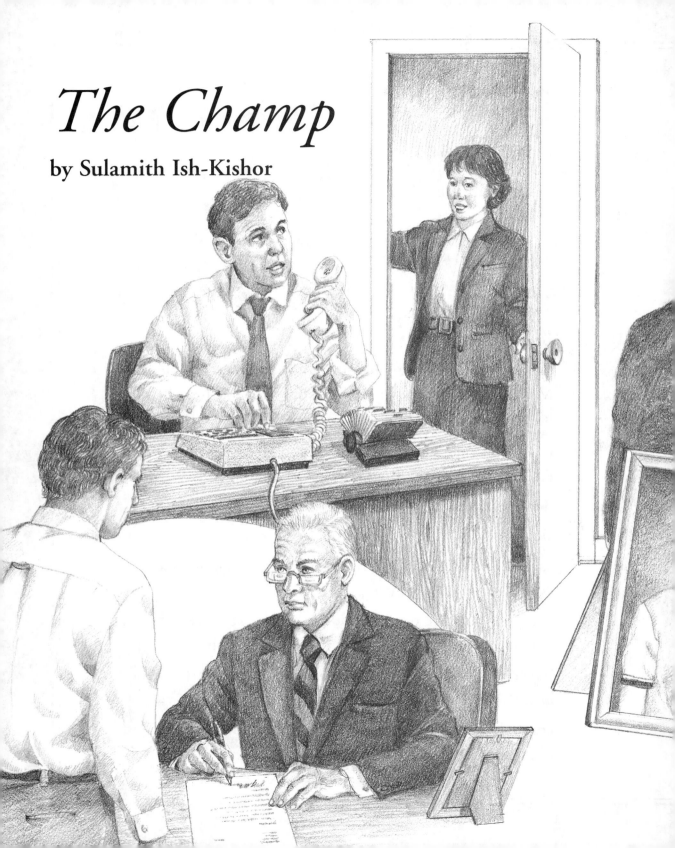

Ben Watson took the train to work. He got there early. He had a lot of things to do. He picked up the telephone. He began to make a call.

Just then there was a knock on the door.

"Yes?" Watson said.

Miss Linn came in. She said, "Mr. Smith wants to see you. He wants to see you right now."

Watson put down the telephone. He got up at once. He walked down the hall. He walked very fast. Mr. Smith was the boss. You did not make him wait.

"Sit down, Watson," said the boss.
Watson sat down.

The boss was at his **desk.** He was reading some papers. He began to sign them.

Watson looked at the boss. Mr. Smith's hair was gray. He had lines in his face. He looked very old. Yes, Mr. Smith looked old. His son had died. That was just three weeks ago.

Poor Herbie Smith! The boy had been sick all his life. It was hard for him to walk. He had to use a cane. Everyone knew that the boy would not live a long life. Only his father did not believe that.

Watson felt sorry for the boss. The boss did his best to save his only son. He did everything he could.

But you could not feel too sorry for Mr. Smith. It was hard to work for him. He only cared about two things. One was his son. Making money was the other.

Mr. Smith made you worry all the time. He had fired many people. He just told them to go. He did not care what they said. He never listened to them.

The boss looked up. He had cold, blue eyes.

"Watson," he said. "Your **department** lost money this year."

Watson felt **weak.** "Yes, sir," he said. "But no one could have done better. Things were different this year. You know how things were."

"Right," said Mr. Smith. "We are closing that department. You will have to go. I am sorry, Watson. You are finished here. Get your things together. This is your last day."

"But, sir," Watson said. "I just need a little more time. I know that things will get better. I am sure that they will! My son goes to Finch College. He is doing so well! I would like to be able to keep him there."

"What? What is that?" said the boss. He looked closely at Watson. "Did you say Finch? I did not know you had a son there. Finch is a very good school. You have to pay a lot to go there. Yes. A lot of money. And you do not make a lot."

"I know that, sir. But he likes it there so much. He is a star runner. And he is the best boxer in the school."

"Ha!" said Mr. Smith. "A champion at everything, I suppose."

Watson's face turned red. "Well, that is what they call him, sir. They call him 'Champ.' They should know."

The boss seemed to turn to stone! He sat very still in his chair. He did not move at all. There was a strange look on his face.

Then the boss stood up. "Look, Watson," he said. "We are closing your department. We will close it today. You will work in another department. You will work longer hours. But you will get much more pay. Now get out. Get out. And do not look for another job. You have a job here for life."

Watson was surprised. What had happened? Why had the boss changed his **mind?** Watson did not know. He did not stay to ask. He quickly went out.

The boss looked through his desk. He took out some letters. He went through the pile. He found the one that he wanted.

It was his son Herbie's last letter. He had sent it from Finch. The boss had read the letter many times. It had always made him feel sad. He read the letter again. This time he felt better.

The letter said:

> I cannot say the boys are nicer to me here. I guess it is the same everywhere. I am different. So some people make fun of me. But do not worry about me, Dad. This is a very good school. And there is one boy here who has really been great. He is a star runner. He is the best boxer in the school. He made them stop picking on me. And he knocked down a boy who hit me, Dad. He is the best friend I ever had. Some day I want to do something for Champ. Something big—that he won't even know about.
>
> Herbie

TELL ABOUT THE STORY.

Put an X in the box next to the right answer. Each answer tells something (a *fact*) about the story.

1. When Mr. Smith called for Watson, Watson went
   - ☐ a. at once.
   - ☐ b. much later.
   - ☐ c. after ten minutes.

2. Watson thought that Mr. Smith looked
   - ☐ a. young.
   - ☐ b. happy.
   - ☐ c. old.

3. At first Mr. Smith said that Watson
   - ☐ a. had to go.
   - ☐ b. could stay there for life.
   - ☐ c. was doing good work.

4. Herbie said that he wanted to
   - ☐ a. leave Finch.
   - ☐ b. do something for Champ.
   - ☐ c. fight some of the boys.

END EACH LINE.

Finish the lines below. Fill in each empty space with one of the words in the box. Each word can be found in the story. There are five words and four empty spaces. This means that one word in the box will not be used.

Most people will work for

_____ than 30 years. That is a
   1

very long _____. So you may
                   2

want to ask yourself, "What are the

_____ I like to do? What kind
   3

of work will _____ me happy?"
                        4

little	more
	make	
time	things

NUMBER CORRECT   X 5 =   YOUR SCORE

NUMBER CORRECT   X 5 =   YOUR SCORE

Show what words mean.

The words below are printed in **dark letters** in the story. You may look back at these vocabulary words before you answer the questions. Put an X in the box next to the right answer.

1. He signed the papers on his desk. A *desk* is a
   - ☐ a. small chair.
   - ☐ b. big book.
   - ☐ c. table used for writing.

2. Watson's department lost money last year. A *department* is
   - ☐ a. a place where people work.
   - ☐ b. someone's house.
   - ☐ c. a neighbor or friend.

3. He was so worried, he began to feel weak. The word *weak* means
   - ☐ a. glad.
   - ☐ b. very tall.
   - ☐ c. not strong.

4. Watson wondered why Mr. Smith changed his mind. As used here, *mind* means
   - ☐ a. what someone wears.
   - ☐ b. what someone thinks.
   - ☐ c. what someone needs.

Think about the story.

Here is how to answer these questions. First think about what happened in the story. Then work out the right answers. This is called *critical thinking*.

1. Which one is true?
   - ☐ a. Herbie did not know Champ.
   - ☐ b. Champ made fun of Herbie.
   - ☐ c. Herbie and Champ were friends.

2. Why did Mr. Smith say that Watson could keep working there?
   - ☐ a. Watson worked very hard.
   - ☐ b. Mr. Smith was always kind.
   - ☐ c. Watson's son helped Herbie.

3. We can guess that Mr. Smith wanted to give Watson more money because Watson
   - ☐ a. asked for more money.
   - ☐ b. needed money for Finch.
   - ☐ c. had no money.

4. At the end of the story, Mr. Smith felt
   - ☐ a. very angry.
   - ☐ b. sadder than ever.
   - ☐ c. happier than before.

	X 5 =	
NUMBER CORRECT		YOUR SCORE

	X 5 =	
NUMBER CORRECT		YOUR SCORE

44

SPOT PARTS OF A STORY.

Stories have **characters**, a **plot**, and a **setting**. (See page 3.) Put an X in the box next to the right answer.

1. What happened last? (**Plot**)
   - ☐ a. Miss Linn came in.
   - ☐ b. Mr. Smith read his son's letter again.
   - ☐ c. Mr. Smith said that Watson was finished.

2. Which best tells about Mr. Smith? (**Character**)
   - ☐ a. He cared a lot about his son.
   - ☐ b. He did not care about his son.
   - ☐ c. He always did what people said.

3. Where does the story take place? (**Setting**)
   - ☐ a. at a school
   - ☐ b. on a train
   - ☐ c. in a room at work

4. When does the story take place? (**Setting**)
   - ☐ a. now
   - ☐ b. a year ago
   - ☐ c. three years ago

```
┌──────┐        ┌──────┐
│      │  x 5 = │      │
└──────┘        └──────┘
NUMBER           YOUR
CORRECT          SCORE
```

THINK SOME MORE ABOUT THE STORY.

Your teacher might want you to write your answers.
- Why was Mr. Smith surprised that Watson's son went to Finch?
- Show how Mr. Smith made his son's last wish come true.
- Do you think it was wrong for people to make fun of Herbie? Why?

Write your scores in the box below. Then write your scores on pages 120 and 121.

```
┌──────┐
│      │  T ELL ABOUT THE STORY
└──────┘
   +
┌──────┐
│      │  E ND EACH LINE
└──────┘
   +
┌──────┐
│      │  S HOW WHAT WORDS MEAN
└──────┘
   +
┌──────┐
│      │  T HINK ABOUT THE STORY
└──────┘
   +
┌──────┐
│      │  S POT PARTS OF A STORY
└──────┘
   =
┌──────┐
│      │  TOTAL SCORE: Story 3
└──────┘
```

4
The Old House

by Judith B. Stamper

Before You Read

Before you read "The Old House," go over the words below. Make sure you know what each word means. This will help you when you read the story.

spend: to pass time. She was going to *spend* the night in the house.

dust: very small pieces of dirt. I could write my name in the *dust* on the table.

blank: empty. There was nothing on the *blank* page.

person: someone—a man, woman, or child. A *person* was coming up the steps.

wrote: put words on a page. The class *wrote* a story.

The Old House

by Judith B. Stamper

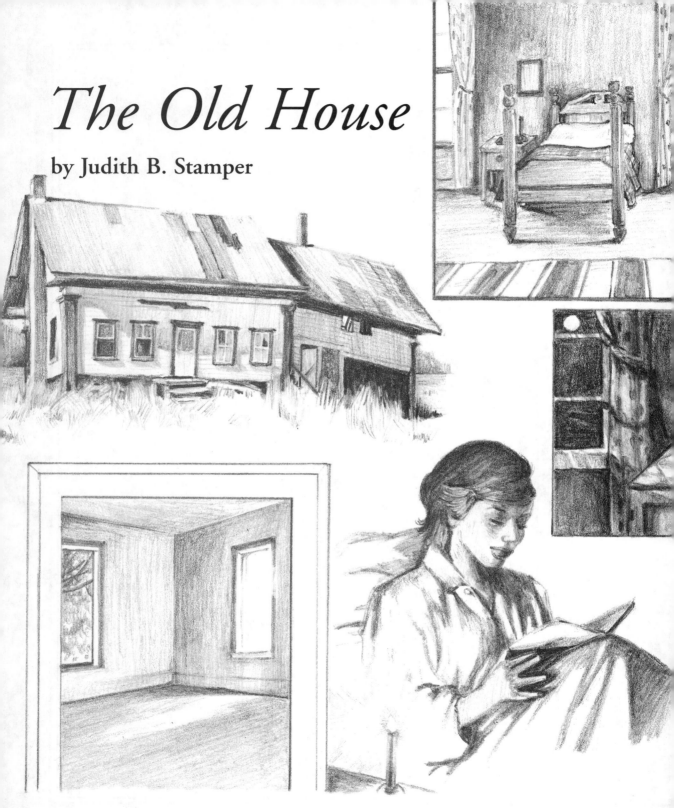

Ann had been driving for a long time. It was getting late. She was tired. Then she came to Elm Street.

"At last!" she thought to herself. "I will be there soon."

Ann turned onto Elm Street. She came to a road. She went to the end of the road. There was the old house!

Ann came closer to the house. She was surprised. They told her the old house was white. But the house was not white. It had once been white. Now the house was gray.

They said that the house was falling down. They were right about that. One side was beginning to **sink**. There were holes in the roof. Many windows were broken.

Ann thought, "Soon this old house will be gone. No one will live here again. But I will stay for the night."

Ann worked for the Stantons. They bought and sold houses. Two weeks ago they bought the old house. They were going to **tear** it down. Then they would sell the land it was on.

Mrs. Stanton said, "We must look at the house one more time. Who wants to go?"

Ann said, "I will go."

Mr. Stanton said, "It is very far from here."

Ann said, "That is all right. I will drive. I can spend the night there."

Mrs. Stanton said, "Are you sure? People say the old house is strange. Funny things happen there."

"I will be fine," Ann said.

Ann looked at the old house. She had said, "I will be fine." Now she was not sure.

Ann went up to the house. She walked up the old steps. They made a sound under her feet. Ann found the key that the Stantons had given her. She put the key in the door. The door slowly opened.

Ann went into the house. The air seemed heavy and old. Ann thought, "How long has it been since someone lived here?"

Ann looked around. There was dust everywhere. Then she opened a door. She saw a small room. She was very surprised. The room was clean! There was no dust anywhere!

There was a bed in the room. Next to the bed was a table. There was a candle on top of the table.

Ann said to herself, "This room will do. I will stay here tonight."

Ann went back to the car. She got her things. Then she went to the room.

It was dark in the room. Ann lighted the candle. Light danced around.

That was when she saw the little book. It was lying on the table.

"That is funny," thought Ann. "It looks as if someone left this for me."

Ann read the name on the book. The book was called *The Old House.*

"*The Old House!* That *is* strange," thought Ann. "I will look at this later."

Ann went outside to take a walk. She walked down the road. She did not hear a sound. No one else was around.

Ann started back to the house. It was hard to see in the dark. She **slipped** on the road. Her leg hit the ground.

Ann sat on the ground. She had hurt her leg. She rested awhile. Then she felt better.

Ann slowly got up. She walked to the house. She went to the room. The candle was still burning. Ann got into the bed.

Then Ann saw the little book. She picked it up. She began to read:

This story is about a young woman. She goes to look at an old house. The house is far away. The woman gets into her car. She drives for a long time. Then she comes to the house. It is late. She is tired. She thinks, "I will stay for the night."

Ann shut the book. She put it down on the table. She closed her eyes. But she could not stop thinking about the book. It was strange. Very strange. Ann tried to sleep. But she kept thinking about the book. What would the book say? What would happen next?

Ann picked up the book. She read some more:

The house is very old. It is nearly falling down. The young woman looks through the house. She finds a small room. It is nicer than the others. She gets her things from the car. Then she goes outside. It is very quiet there. No one else is around. She starts to go back to the house. But she falls in the dark. She hurts her leg.

Ann's leg still hurt. Now it hurt even more. Ann began to feel frightened. Her hands started to shake. She could not hold the book still. Ann looked out the window. She saw the moon in the sky.

Ann tried not to think about the book. But she *had* to know! What was going to happen? What would the book say? She kept on reading:

The young woman sees a little book. It is on the table. The book is called The Old House. She picks up the book. She begins to read. As she reads, she feels frightened. She is afraid. She is afraid that something will happen. She is afraid. But what can she do?

Ann stopped reading. She was afraid. That *was* so. But what *could* she do?

Ann turned to the next page. But it was blank. There was nothing on it. She turned to the next page. That was blank, too. *All* of the pages were blank. The rest of the book was blank!

Ann put the book on the table. She waited. She kept waiting. Yes, she was waiting. She was waiting. But for what?

Then Ann heard a car. It was coming up the road. It was coming to the old house!

Ann did not know what to do. She did not move.

The car stopped. She heard the car door close. She heard someone coming up the front steps. She heard a key in the door.

Ann quickly **grabbed** the book. She turned to a blank page. She began to write:

> The young woman hears a car. It stops at the old house. She hears someone coming up the steps. She hears a key in the door.

Ann heard a noise. Someone was in the house! She heard steps. They were coming closer.

Ann began to write again:

> The young woman hears a noise. Someone is in the house. She hears steps. They are coming closer.

Ann turned the page. She wrote as fast as she could:

But the steps suddenly stop! The person turns around! The person goes back to the car! The young woman waits. She hears the car start. Then she hears the car drive away.

Ann listened. She heard steps. Then the steps stopped. Ann waited. She heard the car start. Then she heard it drive away.

Ann was not shaking now. She picked up *The Old House.* She wrote two more words. They were The End.

Then Ann went to sleep.

TELL ABOUT THE STORY.

Put an X in the box next to the right answer. Each answer tells something (a *fact*) about the story.

1. Ann saw that the old house
   - ☐ a. was falling down.
   - ☐ b. had a beautiful roof.
   - ☐ c. had new windows.

2. When Ann fell, she
   - ☐ a. hit her head.
   - ☐ b. hurt her arm.
   - ☐ c. hurt her leg.

3. Ann kept reading the book because she
   - ☐ a. was not tired.
   - ☐ b. wanted to see what would happen.
   - ☐ c. had nothing else to do.

4. When Ann heard someone coming up the steps, she began to
   - ☐ a. run away.
   - ☐ b. write in the book.
   - ☐ c. hide in the house.

END EACH LINE.

Finish the lines below. Fill in each empty space with one of the words in the box. Each word can be found in the story. There are five words and four empty spaces. This means that one word in the box will not be used.

When you _____ books,
              1
you are never alone. You meet all
kinds of _____. You visit
              2
_____ different places. New
     3
worlds open for you as you ask,
"What will happen _____?"
                        4

door		many
	people	
next		read

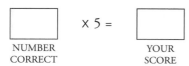

NUMBER CORRECT   X 5 =   YOUR SCORE

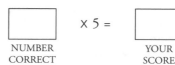

NUMBER CORRECT   X 5 =   YOUR SCORE

SHOW WHAT WORDS MEAN.

The words below are printed in **dark letters** in the story. You may look back at these vocabulary words before you answer the questions. Put an X in the box next to the right answer.

1. The house was beginning to sink into the ground. The word *sink* means
   - ☐ a. stand still.
   - ☐ b. go down.
   - ☐ c. move from side to side.

2. They were going to tear down the house. As used here, *tear* means
   - ☐ a. break down.
   - ☐ b. look at.
   - ☐ c. build.

3. Ann slipped in the dark. The word *slipped* means
   - ☐ a. worried.
   - ☐ b. called.
   - ☐ c. fell.

4. She quickly grabbed the book. The word *grabbed* means
   - ☐ a. threw away.
   - ☐ b. took suddenly.
   - ☐ c. lost.

THINK ABOUT THE STORY.

Here is how to answer these questions. First think about what happened in the story. Then work out the right answers. This is called *critical thinking*.

1. What was strange?
   - ☐ a. The house was very old.
   - ☐ b. One room in the house was clean.
   - ☐ c. Windows were broken.

2. What surprised Ann the most?
   - ☐ a. The house was far away.
   - ☐ b. No one was in the house.
   - ☐ c. She found a book called *The Old House.*

3. We can guess that Ann made the person go away by
   - ☐ a. calling for help.
   - ☐ b. frightening the person away.
   - ☐ c. writing that the person went away.

4. It is fair to say that the young woman in the book was
   - ☐ a. Ann.
   - ☐ b. one of Ann's friends.
   - ☐ c. Mrs. Stanton.

☐ X 5 = ☐

NUMBER CORRECT   YOUR SCORE

☐ X 5 = ☐

NUMBER CORRECT   YOUR SCORE

SPOT PARTS OF A STORY.

Stories have **characters**, a **plot**, and a **setting**. (See page 3.) Put an X in the box next to the right answer.

1. What happened first? (**Plot**)
   - ☐ a. Ann found a book in the house.
   - ☐ b. Ann turned onto Elm Street.
   - ☐ c. Ann hurt her leg.

2. What happened last? (**Plot**)
   - ☐ a. Ann heard the car drive away.
   - ☐ b. Ann walked down the road.
   - ☐ c. Ann heard someone coming up the steps.

3. When does the story take place? (**Setting**)
   - ☐ a. now
   - ☐ b. about five years ago
   - ☐ c. a long time ago

4. Where does the story take place? (**Setting**)
   - ☐ a. in a car
   - ☐ b. on a farm
   - ☐ c. in an old house

THINK SOME MORE ABOUT THE STORY.

Your teacher might want you to write your answers.

- Many strange things happened in the story. What were some of them?
- What did Ann do so that nothing bad happened to her?
- Why do you think Ann wrote the words "The End" in the book?

Write your scores in the box below. Then write your scores on pages 120 and 121.

☐ +
TELL ABOUT THE STORY

☐ +
END EACH LINE

☐ +
SHOW WHAT WORDS MEAN

☐ +
THINK ABOUT THE STORY

☐ =
SPOT PARTS OF A STORY

☐
TOTAL SCORE: **Story 4**

☐ X 5 = ☐

NUMBER CORRECT   YOUR SCORE

5
A Hard World

by Dion Henderson

Before You Read

Before you read "A Hard World," go over the words
below. Make sure you know what each word means. This
will help you when you read the story.

cage: a place to keep animals. They kept the dog in a *cage*.

newspaper: printed pages that give news about things that
have happened. My sister reads the *newspaper* every day.

gifts: things you give to other people. I got many *gifts* for
my birthday.

nodded: moved the head up and down to say yes. Ravi
nodded when I asked him if I could use the car.

A Hard World

by Dion Henderson

Lass was a good dog. She was glad when you gave her food. She was happy. She **wagged** her tail.

Skip, Pal, and Rollo were good dogs too. *All* of our dogs were good. Only Brute was not good.

Brute was not like the other dogs. He was not glad when you gave him food. I put the food into a dish. Then I put the dish into his cage. Brute would look at the food. He would **growl** at me. He would go into a corner. He waited until I went away. Then he ate the food.

I tried to make friends with Brute. But Brute did not want to be friends. He wanted you to leave him alone. You could *make* him do things. But it was hard work.

My wife, Betty, and I lived in the hills. We had a lot of dogs. We brought them up. We took care of them. We sold most of the dogs. We made our living that way.

One evening Betty said, "Tom, did you send someone down to the cages today?"

"No," I said. "Why?"

"I thought I saw someone there. It looked like a boy."

I said, "A boy brings the newspaper. Maybe he stopped to look at the dogs. The new puppies are there. Maybe he stopped to look at them."

"Maybe," Betty said. "It might have been him."

The next morning I went to the cages. Some of the doors were open. I looked at the puppies. They were all there. Brute barked at me. Then he went to his corner. I wondered if he had **scared** someone away.

I closed the cage doors. Then I did my work.

Betty and I sat around after dinner. We talked about the open cages. Someone could have taken the puppies. That was easy to do. But we had never had any trouble before.

Two days later, we heard some noise. I put on my coat. I went outside. I went down to the cages.

Lass was barking. The puppies were jumping up and down. I counted the puppies. They were all there. Then I saw the open door. Brute was gone!

That night someone knocked on our door. He was a tall man. He had a boy with him.

I knew who the man was. He had moved here about a year ago. He did some farming. But he was having a hard time. He did not make much money.

"Come in, Sam," I said. "Why don't you sit down?"

"No, thank you," said Sam. "We will not stay long."

He looked at the boy. "Jed here has something to say."

"Yes, sir," said Jed. "I—I—I took your dog. I took him. I am sorry."

I was surprised. I said, "But there were some good dogs in the cages. You did not take *them.*"

Jed said, "I took a good dog!" He looked at me. "Some people do not know a good dog when they see one."

"Jed!" said Sam. "Watch what you say!"

"Yes, sir," said the boy.

I asked, "Where is the dog now?"

"I will get him," said the boy.

The boy whistled. Then Brute came running up the road. He was wagging his tail! The boy **patted** Brute's head. Brute put his face against the boy's hand!

The boy began to cry softly. He **patted** Brute some more. Then the boy ran down the road.

The dog started to follow him. The boy turned around. "Go back! Go back!" he called to the dog. And Brute went back! Brute listened to him!

I could not believe what I saw. I saw Brute wag his tail! I saw Brute put his face against the boy's hand! I could not believe what I saw!

Sam was still standing there. He said, "Is there anything else we should do?"

"No," I said. "It is all right now. I will stop by your house some time. Maybe we can talk."

"Come by if you want to," he said.

I thought about what had happened. I thought, "Maybe I should give Brute to the boy." But I knew the kind of man Jed's father was. He would not take something for nothing.

I was right. I let three days go by. Then I went to see Sam. We talked for a long time. He told me some things about Jed and Brute. Then I said, "Jed can have Brute."

"No, Tom," he said. "We do not take gifts. I know you can sell the dog. Thank you very much. But do not talk to me about this again. This is a hard world. Jed must find that out sooner or later."

"Yes," I said. "This is a hard world." Then I went home.

I got home a little later. I went to the cages. I looked at Brute. I saw he was sad. In a way, that was good. I thought, "It means there is someone he cares about."

I wished that Jed could have the dog. That would be good for Jed. It would be good for Brute. But there was nothing I could do. You cannot make a man like Sam do what he does not want to do.

I went into the house. Betty was there. I told her what Sam had told me. Jed had been coming to the cages. He came there all fall. He came there all winter. He talked to Brute every day. Jed took Brute away with him once. But Jed brought him back later. Jed came back the next day. He took Brute again. Sam found out. That night he made Jed bring the dog to our house.

Some time went by. One night there was a knock on the door. Sam was there.

He said, "Can I have a word with you now? I know it is late."

I said, "It is all right. A word about what?"

"I—I was hoping you might sell me the dog."

I did not answer at once. I wanted to say the right thing.

"I might," I said. "If you give me what is fair."

He seemed glad I said that. "Good," he said. "I was afraid you would try to give him away."

I nodded my head. That seemed to be the best thing to do.

He said, "I brought some money with me. I do not know how much you want. But I brought what I thought was right."

He held out the money.

I waited a minute. Then I said, "That is fair." And I guess it was.

"Done!" he said. Then he smiled a little.

"You know," he said, "Jed's birthday is tomorrow. That is all the money we had for a present for him. But nothing else would make Jed happy."

I put on my coat. Then we walked to the cages.

Sam said, "We wanted our son to be happy on his birthday."

"Well," I said. "It is a hard world. He will find that out sooner or later."

"Yes," Sam said. "It *is* a hard world. But he can find that out a little at a time."

I opened the door of Brute's cage. Brute quietly came out. He walked down the road with Sam. I watched them until they were gone.

TELL ABOUT THE STORY.

Put an X in the box next to the right answer. Each answer tells something (a *fact*) about the story.

1. Tom and Betty made a living by
   - ☐ a. cutting down trees.
   - ☐ b. working as farmers.
   - ☐ c. selling dogs.

2. Jed told Tom that he
   - ☐ a. took Tom's dog.
   - ☐ b. thought Brute was a bad dog.
   - ☐ c. wanted to buy Brute.

3. Tom was surprised that Brute
   - ☐ a. ate so much.
   - ☐ b. was like the other dogs.
   - ☐ c. put his face against Jed's hand.

4. Jed talked to Brute
   - ☐ a. only two or three times.
   - ☐ b. all fall and winter.
   - ☐ c. most of the summer.

END EACH LINE.

Finish the lines below. Fill in each empty space with one of the words in the box. Each word can be found in the story. There are five words and four empty spaces. This means that one word in the box will not be used.

Some _____ help people
                1
who cannot see. These dogs are

_____ Seeing Eye dogs. Seeing
      2
Eye dogs make sure that people do

not _____ into things. The
            3
dogs let people go across the street

only _____ it is safe.
              4

called	when
dogs	
road	walk

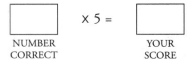

NUMBER CORRECT   x 5 =   YOUR SCORE

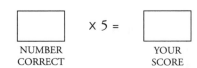

NUMBER CORRECT   x 5 =   YOUR SCORE

73

SHOW WHAT WORDS MEAN.

The words below are printed in **dark letters** in the story. You may look back at these vocabulary words before you answer the questions. Put an X in the box next to the right answer.

1. The dog wagged his tail. The word *wagged* means
   - ☐ a. moved from side to side.
   - ☐ b. tried to find.
   - ☐ c. hit the ground.

2. Brute started to growl when Tom came near. The word *growl* means
   - ☐ a. to eat a lot.
   - ☐ b. to make an angry sound.
   - ☐ c. to jump into the air.

3. He thought that Brute scared someone away. The word *scared* means
   - ☐ a. made someone sad.
   - ☐ b. made someone happy.
   - ☐ c. made someone afraid.

4. Jed patted Brute's head. The word *patted* means
   - ☐ a. put a hand on lightly.
   - ☐ b. pushed very hard.
   - ☐ c. gave some food.

☐ **× 5 =** ☐

NUMBER CORRECT   YOUR SCORE

THINK ABOUT THE STORY.

Here is how to answer these questions. First think about what happened in the story. Then work out the right answers. This is called *critical thinking*.

1. We may guess that Brute listened to Jed because Jed
   - ☐ a. beat him.
   - ☐ b. shouted at him.
   - ☐ c. talked to him so often.

2. What surprised Tom the most?
   - ☐ a. Brute came when Jed whistled.
   - ☐ b. Lass was glad when you gave her food.
   - ☐ c. Sam did some farming.

3. Which one is true?
   - ☐ a. Tom liked Brute a lot.
   - ☐ b. Sam thought his son had time to find out that the world was hard.
   - ☐ c. Jed did not like Brute.

4. When he got Brute as a present, Jed must have felt
   - ☐ a. very happy.
   - ☐ b. angry.
   - ☐ c. sad.

☐ **× 5 =** ☐

NUMBER CORRECT   YOUR SCORE

SPOT PARTS OF A STORY.

Stories have **characters**, a **plot**, and a **setting**. (See page 3.) Put an X in the box next to the right answer.

1. What happened last? (**Plot**)
   - ☐ a. Betty thought she saw a boy by the cages.
   - ☐ b. Sam bought Brute.
   - ☐ c. Jed went to Sam's house.

2. Which best tells about Jed? (**Character**)
   - ☐ a. He loved Brute.
   - ☐ b. He never listened to his father.
   - ☐ c. He did not like animals.

3. Which best tells about Sam? (**Character**)
   - ☐ a. He did not work hard.
   - ☐ b. He made a lot of money.
   - ☐ c. He did not want something for nothing.

4. Where does the story take place? (**Setting**)
   - ☐ a. in the middle of a city
   - ☐ b. somewhere in the hills
   - ☐ c. in a store

THINK SOME MORE ABOUT THE STORY.

Your teacher might want you to write your answers.
- Jed took Brute and not some other dog. Why did this surprise Tom?
- Brute listened to Jed and did not listen to Tom. Why? What does that show?
- Sam would not take Brute without paying for him. Why?

Write your scores in the box below. Then write your scores on pages 120 and 121.

☐ +	**T**ELL ABOUT THE STORY
☐ +	**E**ND EACH LINE
☐ +	**S**HOW WHAT WORDS MEAN
☐ +	**T**HINK ABOUT THE STORY
☐ =	**S**POT PARTS OF A STORY
☐	TOTAL SCORE: **Story 5**

☐ × 5 = ☐

NUMBER CORRECT   YOUR SCORE

75

6
Yes I Can

a story from West Africa

Before You Read

Before you read "Yes I Can," go over the words below. Make sure you know what each word means. This will help you when you read the story.

storyteller: someone who tells stories. The *storyteller* told a funny story.

danger: something that can hurt you. The bird was in *danger* when the cat came near it.

skin: Skin covers the outside of the body. The hot sun burned Maria's *skin*.

yelling: calling out. They kept *yelling,* "Go away!"

Yes I Can

a story from West Africa

Noma was a very good storyteller. She was the best storyteller in Accra. That is a town in West Africa.

Noma had a sister. Her name was Tok. One day Noma and Tok were visiting their aunt. She lived in a village. It was near Accra.

Noma and Tok had dinner with their aunt. It began to get late. They said goodbye to their aunt. Then they started to walk home.

They talked as they walked. Tok said, "Noma. You tell stories very well. You are the best storyteller in Accra. How many stories do you know?"

"Oh," said Noma. "I know a lot. I like to make up stories. Making up stories is fun."

"Yes," said Tok. "But most of your stories are about animals. Why is that so?"

"I *like* animals," said Noma. "Do you know the story about the rabbit and the monkey?"

"No," said Tok. "Tell it to me."

"All right," said Noma.

This is the story Noma told.

A monkey lived in a tall tree. A rabbit lived in a field near the tree. The monkey and the rabbit met now and then. They talked to each other.

You know that rabbits have very long ears. Rabbits can hear very well. They can hear anything that is near. So a rabbit turns its head all the time. The rabbit is listening. It wants to be sure there is no danger near.

One day the monkey and the rabbit were talking. The monkey was talking about his children. The monkey liked to talk about his children. He talked about them all the time.

The monkey said, "My children moved away. They do not visit us too often. But they are doing very well. Oh, yes. They are doing very, very well."

The rabbit had no children. He had heard the story before. He was not listening to the monkey. But the rabbit heard noises. He kept turning his head. He turned it to the left. He turned it to the right. He turned his head from side to side.

The monkey got angry. "Friend rabbit!" said the monkey. "How can I *talk* to you? You keep moving your head!"

Then the rabbit got angry. He said, "Friend monkey! How can I *listen* to you? You keep **scratching** your skin!"

That was so. A rabbit keeps turning its head. But a monkey keeps scratching its skin. A monkey scratches its head. Then it scratches its arms and its back. That is the way monkeys are.

The monkey said, "Well! *I* can stop scratching my skin! But *you* cannot stop turning your head!"

The rabbit said, "Yes I can! *I* can stop turning my head. But *you* cannot stop scratching your skin!"

The monkey said, "Yes I can!"

"We will see!" said the rabbit.

"We will see!" said the monkey.

So they stood next to each other. They stood for a long time. They did not say a word.

The rabbit heard noises. He heard noises all around him. The noises got louder. They got louder and louder. But he did not turn his head.

The rabbit *wanted* to turn his head. Oh, how he wanted to turn it! Oh, if *only* he could turn it! But he did not turn his head.

And the monkey? He felt **awful.** Oh, how his skin was burning! Oh, how badly it was burning! How he wanted to scratch it! If only he could scratch it! But he did not scratch his skin.

Oh, that poor monkey!

Oh, that poor rabbit!

They kept looking at each other! They kept watching each other!

The rabbit **finally** said, "Friend monkey. We may be here for a while. Let me tell you a story. It will make the time go faster."

The monkey's skin was burning. He was glad to hear a story. He thought, "A story cannot hurt me. But maybe it can help me."

So he said, "Friend Rabbit. Tell me your story."

"Well, then," said the rabbit. "Last week I went to a field. It was the field next to this one."

"Yes," said the monkey, "I know that field well."

The rabbit said, "There are many good things to eat in that field. I got there early in the morning. I was in the tall grass. I heard a noise. The noise came from my left. I looked to my left."

The rabbit turned his head to the left. Oh, my that felt good!

"I heard a noise to my right," said the rabbit.

The rabbit turned his head to the right. Oh, my that felt good!

"There were noises all *around,*" said the rabbit.

The rabbit kept turning his head. Oh, my that felt good!

"Yes!" said the monkey. "I was right behind you that day! I saw the farmer and his sons. The farmer's wife was there, too. They were yelling at you. Then they started to throw stones. The stones went over your head. One stone hit me *right here!*"

The monkey **slapped** his head. Oh, my that felt good!

"Another stone hit me *right here.*" The monkey slapped his arm. Oh, my that felt good!

"Another stone hit me *here.*" The monkey slapped his back. Oh, my that felt good!

The rabbit had to smile. "Friend monkey," he said, "I see you liked my story."

"Yes," the monkey smiled back. "I liked it just as much as *you* did!"

"I liked that story, too," said Tok.

"Good," Noma said. "And look! We are home!"

She pushed open the door. And they went into the house.

TELL ABOUT THE STORY.

Put an X in the box next to the right answer. Each answer tells something (a *fact*) about the story.

1. Noma said that she knew
   - [ ] a. one or two stories.
   - [ ] b. just a few stories.
   - [ ] c. many stories.

2. The monkey liked to talk about
   - [ ] a. his children.
   - [ ] b. the rabbit.
   - [ ] c. his friends.

3. The rabbit wanted to
   - [ ] a. visit the monkey.
   - [ ] b. turn its head.
   - [ ] c. hear Noma's story.

4. The monkey said he was hit by
   - [ ] a. a falling tree.
   - [ ] b. another monkey.
   - [ ] c. stones.

END EACH LINE.

Finish the lines below. Fill in each empty space with one of the words in the box. Each word can be found in the story. There are five words and four empty spaces. This means that one word in the box will not be used.

Did you _____ these things 1 about rabbits? Rabbits can run very _____. But they cannot run 2 fast for a _____ time. Rabbits 3 can swim. They are also able to move both _____ at once. 4

story	ears
	fast	
know	long

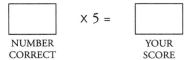

NUMBER CORRECT   X 5 =   YOUR SCORE

NUMBER CORRECT   X 5 =   YOUR SCORE

SHOW WHAT WORDS MEAN.

The words below are printed in **dark letters** in the story. You may look back at these vocabulary words before you answer the questions. Put an X in the box next to the right answer.

1. The monkey kept scratching its head. The word *scratching* means
   - ☐ a. rubbing.
   - ☐ b. thinking.
   - ☐ c. holding.

2. The monkey and the rabbit both felt awful. The word *awful* means
   - ☐ a. very good.
   - ☐ b. very bad.
   - ☐ c. very old.

3. The rabbit finally talked to the monkey. The word *finally* means
   - ☐ a. after a while.
   - ☐ b. never.
   - ☐ c. often.

4. The monkey slapped his head. The word *slapped* means
   - ☐ a. looked at.
   - ☐ b. fell on.
   - ☐ c. hit with the hand.

THINK ABOUT THE STORY.

Here is how to answer these questions. First think about what happened in the story. Then work out the right answers. This is called *critical thinking*.

1. The rabbit told the story to
   - ☐ a. move his head.
   - ☐ b. help the monkey.
   - ☐ c. make fun of the monkey.

2. It is fair to say that the monkey
   - ☐ a. never saw his children.
   - ☐ b. met the rabbit often.
   - ☐ c. used the rabbit's story to help himself.

3. Which one is true?
   - ☐ a. Tok knew the story about the rabbit and the monkey.
   - ☐ b. Noma liked to make up stories.
   - ☐ c. Most of Noma's stories were about people.

4. "Yes I Can" shows that it is
   - ☐ a. easy to change what you always do.
   - ☐ b. hard to change what you always do.
   - ☐ c. hard to tell stories.

☐ × 5 = ☐

NUMBER CORRECT   YOUR SCORE

☐ × 5 = ☐

NUMBER CORRECT   YOUR SCORE

SPOT PARTS OF A STORY.

Stories have **characters,** a **plot,** and a **setting.** (See page 3.) Put an X in the box next to the right answer.

1. What happened first? (**Plot**)
   - ☐ a. Noma told Tok a story.
   - ☐ b. Noma and Tok came home.
   - ☐ c. Noma and Tok visited their aunt.

2. Which best tells about Noma? (**Character**)
   - ☐ a. She told stories very well.
   - ☐ b. She did not like to make up stories.
   - ☐ c. She did not like animals.

3. Which best tells about the rabbit? (**Character**)
   - ☐ a. He had many children.
   - ☐ b. He turned his head all the time.
   - ☐ c. He always listened to the monkey's stories.

4. Where does the story take place? (**Setting**)
   - ☐ a. in East Asia
   - ☐ b. in West Africa
   - ☐ c. in North America

☐ ✕ 5 = ☐

NUMBER CORRECT   YOUR SCORE

THINK SOME MORE ABOUT THE STORY.

Your teacher might want you to write your answers.
- Why did the rabbit tell the story to the monkey?
- Do you think the monkey was really in the field with the rabbit? Tell why.
- Why do you think the story is called "Yes I Can"?

Write your scores in the box below. Then write your scores on pages 120 and 121.

☐ **T**ELL ABOUT THE STORY
+
☐ **E**ND EACH LINE
+
☐ **S**HOW WHAT WORDS MEAN
+
☐ **T**HINK ABOUT THE STORY
+
☐ **S**POT PARTS OF A STORY
=
☐ TOTAL SCORE: **Story 6**

7

The Long Sleep

by Lin Yutang

Before You Read

Before you read "The Long Sleep," go over the words below. Make sure you know what each word means. This will help you when you read the story.

doctors: people who help others get well and stay well. The *doctors* told Jan to rest for a week.

slept: was sleeping or had been sleeping. Carlos dreamed while he *slept*.

worm: a small, soft animal that has no legs. The bird found a *worm*.

knife: something used for cutting. My teacher cut the cake with a *knife*.

The Long Sleep

by Lin Yutang

This story is very old. It comes from China. It was told there more than 1000 years ago.

Long ago, Cho owned a store. It was in Meng. That is a city in China.

Three men worked in Cho's store. Their names were Sung, Wu, and Kwok. Cho was friendly with them. They liked Cho too. They did what Cho said. After all, they worked for Cho. He gave them money.

One day Cho did not feel well. He got into bed. Cho did not eat. He did not drink. He did not move. He just stayed in bed.

Cho's wife, Li, was worried. She called for some doctors. They came to the house. They looked at Cho. They all said the same thing. They said, "We know Cho is sick. But we do not know why. We do not know what to do. We cannot help Cho."

Cho said, "I feel tired."

Then Cho fell asleep. He kept on sleeping. He slept for 10 days.

Suddenly Cho sat up. He opened his eyes. He saw his wife. He said, "How long did I sleep?"

Li said, "You were asleep for a long time. You were asleep for 10 days."

"Ten days," said Cho. "That is what I thought. What day is today?"

She said, "It is Sunday."

Cho said, "That is what I thought. What time is it now?"

Li said, "It is dinner time. It is nearly six o'clock."

Cho said, "Dear wife. Please go to Sung's house. See if Wu and Kwok are there. See if Sung is making dinner. See if they are going to have fish. If they are, they must all leave. They must come here at once. I have something to tell them."

Li went to Sung's house. Wu and Kwok came to the door.

Li said, "Why are you here?"

They said, "Sung is making dinner for us."

She said, "What will you eat?"

They said, "We will have fish."

Li said, "Come with me now. Sung must come too. You must see Cho at once. He has something to tell you."

They were surprised to see Li. But they were glad that Cho was **awake.** They went to see Cho.

"Good day," Cho told his friends. "I am happy to see you."

Cho turned to Sung. Cho said, "Listen to me. Do not say a word until I have finished."

Everyone waited. What would Cho say?

Cho said, "Sung, you wanted to make dinner for Wu and Kwok. You wanted to make fish. So you went to the store. You wanted a big fish. But you did not see a fish that you liked. The man at the store said, 'Go down to the river. You can buy a fish there.'

"You went to the river. A fishing boat came in. A man got off the boat. The man was very tall. The man had red hair. He was wearing a brown coat.

"He had caught some big fish. You found one you liked. You gave money to the man. Then you took the fish home. Wu and Kwok came to your house. You showed them the fish. Then my wife knocked on your door."

Cho looked at Sung. Cho said, "Is all of that so? Is it just as I said?"

Sung was very surprised. "Yes!" Sung said. "It *all* happened that way! But how did you know? You were in bed. How *could* you know?"

This is what Cho said:

"I was not feeling well. I got into bed. Doctors came. I do not know what they said. But my head felt hot. It got hotter and hotter. I closed my eyes. I fell fast asleep.

"I was asleep. But still I felt hot. I thought 'I will go for a walk. I will walk by the river. It is cool by the river.'

"So I got up. I went outside. I walked to the river. I was right. It was much cooler there.

"I looked at the water. The water was so blue. How beautiful it was!

"Suddenly I thought, 'I would like to swim in the water.'

"So I took off my shoes. I jumped into the water. Down, down I went. There was water all around me. I started to swim.

"I thought, 'This is fun. It is too bad about Sung, Wu, and Kwok. They have to work. I have to work too. I wish that I could be a fish. How happy I would be! I would have nothing to do. I could swim all the time. Oh, I wish I were a fish!'

"A fish **swam** up to me. It said, 'You can be a fish. Is that what you want? Do you want to be a fish?'

"'Yes,' I said, 'I want to be a fish. I just want to swim.'

"'Very well,' said the fish. 'Now you are a fish!'

"I looked down at myself. I saw I had changed. I was a fish!"

"So I was a fish. I liked being a fish. I liked to swim day after day. But one day I was hungry. I looked everywhere. I could not find any food.

"I saw a worm in the water. It looked good to eat. I said to myself, 'Do not eat that worm. If you do, you will be caught. Stay away from that worm!'

"But I was very hungry. I ate the worm. And so I was caught!

"A man pulled me up. He was in a boat. The man was very tall. The man had red hair. He was wearing a brown coat.

"I told the man, 'My name is Cho. I own a store. You must let me go!' But the man did not hear me.

"He put me with some other fish. There was nothing I could do. So I just waited there.

"Then Sung came by. I heard Sung talking to the man. Sung gave money to the man. The man put me in a bag. The man gave me to Sung.

"I said, 'Sung! It is me! I am Cho! You work in my store. What are you doing? Sung! Let me go!'

"But Sung did not hear me. Sung **brought** me home. He went into the kitchen. He took me out of the bag. Sung looked at me. He said, 'You are a beautiful fish.'

"Well! You can guess how I felt!

"Wu and Kwok came by later. Sung showed me to them. He said, 'We will eat this fish soon.'

"I said, 'Friends! It is me! It is Cho! You cannot do this to me!'

"But nobody heard me.

"Just then there was a knock on the door. Wu and Kwok went to the door. They saw my wife. She began talking to them. Then they called out to Sung. They said, 'You must come right away!'

"Sung said, 'I will be there in a minute.'

"Sung put me on the kitchen table. He picked up his knife.

"'Sung!' I cried out. 'I am Cho! I am Cho! Please do not kill me!'

"The knife started to come down. I saw it over my head. Just then I woke up. I was home in my bed!"

No one said a word. Then Wu said, "That was a strange dream."

They were quiet again.

Then Sung said, "Now I **remember.** I saw the fish's mouth move. But I did not hear a sound."

Cho felt better the next day. He went to work. His friends did not say a word about Cho's dream. But they never ate fish again.

TELL ABOUT THE STORY.

Put an X in the box next to the right answer. Each answer tells something (a *fact*) about the story.

1. Cho was asleep for
   - ☐ a. 10 days.
   - ☐ b. two weeks.
   - ☐ c. 10 weeks.

2. Sung bought the fish
   - ☐ a. at a store.
   - ☐ b. from a neighbor.
   - ☐ c. from a man in a boat.

3. Li told Cho's friends to
   - ☐ a. eat dinner.
   - ☐ b. go to Cho at once.
   - ☐ c. go to the store.

4. Cho told a story about how he
   - ☐ a. had a fight with a man.
   - ☐ b. became a fish.
   - ☐ c. was helped by his doctors.

END EACH LINE.

Finish the lines below. Fill in each empty space with one of the words in the box. Each word can be found in the story. There are five words and four empty spaces. This means that one word in the box will not be used.

When you sleep, you do not stay still all _____. You

1

_____ your arms and your

2

legs. You also move your _____.

3

Most people move from one side to another more than _____

4

times a night.

head		ten
	think	
night		move

☐	× 5 =	☐
NUMBER CORRECT		YOUR SCORE

☐	× 5 =	☐
NUMBER CORRECT		YOUR SCORE

SHOW WHAT WORDS MEAN.

The words below are printed in **dark letters** in the story. You may look back at these vocabulary words before you answer the questions. Put an X in the box next to the right answer.

1. Cho opened his eyes and was awake. The word *awake* means
   - ☐ a. not well.
   - ☐ b. not sleeping.
   - ☐ c. surprised.

2. A fish swam up to him. The word *swam* means
   - ☐ a. waited a long time
   - ☐ b. moved along in the water.
   - ☐ c. gave some food.

3. He brought the fish home with him. The word *brought* means
   - ☐ a. took.
   - ☐ b. saw.
   - ☐ c. wanted.

4. Sung was able to remember what happened. The word *remember* means
   - ☐ a. to like.
   - ☐ b. to help.
   - ☐ c. to think about again.

THINK ABOUT THE STORY.

Here is how to answer these questions. First think about what happened in the story. Then work out the right answers. This is called *critical thinking*.

1. When Cho saw the knife come down, he
   - ☐ a. woke up.
   - ☐ b. was not afraid.
   - ☐ c. asked Li to help him.

2. Cho's friends were surprised he
   - ☐ a. gave them money.
   - ☐ b. walked near the river.
   - ☐ c. knew about Sung and the fish.

3. Which one is true?
   - ☐ a. Cho really turned into a fish.
   - ☐ b. The day after his dream, Cho felt better.
   - ☐ c. The doctors helped Cho.

4. The strange thing about the story is that
   - ☐ a. Cho did not feel well.
   - ☐ b. Cho owned a store.
   - ☐ c. so many things in Cho's dream really happened.

☐ X 5 = ☐
NUMBER CORRECT   YOUR SCORE

☐ X 5 = ☐
NUMBER CORRECT   YOUR SCORE

SPOT PARTS OF A STORY.

Stories have **characters**, a **plot**, and a **setting**. (See page 3.) Put an X in the box next to the right answer.

1. What happened first? (**Plot**)
   - ☐ a. Li went to Sung's house.
   - ☐ b. Sung bought a big fish.
   - ☐ c. Some doctors looked at Cho.

2. What happened last? (**Plot**)
   - ☐ a. Cho jumped into the water.
   - ☐ b. Wu said, "That was a strange dream."
   - ☐ c. Sung showed the fish to his friends.

3. Where does the story take place? (**Setting**)
   - ☐ a. Russia
   - ☐ b. China
   - ☐ c. Japan

4. When does the story take place? (**Setting**)
   - ☐ a. a year ago
   - ☐ b. a few years ago
   - ☐ c. long ago

THINK SOME MORE ABOUT THE STORY.

Your teacher might want you to write your answers.

- Many strange things happened in the story. What were some of them?
- Why do you think Cho's friends did not say a word about Cho's dream?
- Why do you think Cho's friends never ate fish again?

Write your scores in the box below. Then write your scores on pages 120 and 121.

☐ **T**ELL ABOUT THE STORY
+
☐ **E**ND EACH LINE
+
☐ **S**HOW WHAT WORDS MEAN
+
☐ **T**HINK ABOUT THE STORY
+
☐ **S**POT PARTS OF A STORY
=
☐ TOTAL SCORE: **Story 7**

☐ X 5 = ☐

NUMBER CORRECT   YOUR SCORE

8
The Driver

by Sinclair Lewis

Before You Read

Before you read "The Driver," go over the words below. Make sure you know what each word means. This will help you when you read the story.

law: A law tells people what they can or cannot do. The *law* says you must stop at a red light.

hour: 60 minutes. I read the book for an *hour*.

fellow: man or boy. That *fellow* is my brother.

tip: money you give to someone who has helped you. Please give a *tip* to the man who carried the bags.

The Driver

by Sinclair Lewis

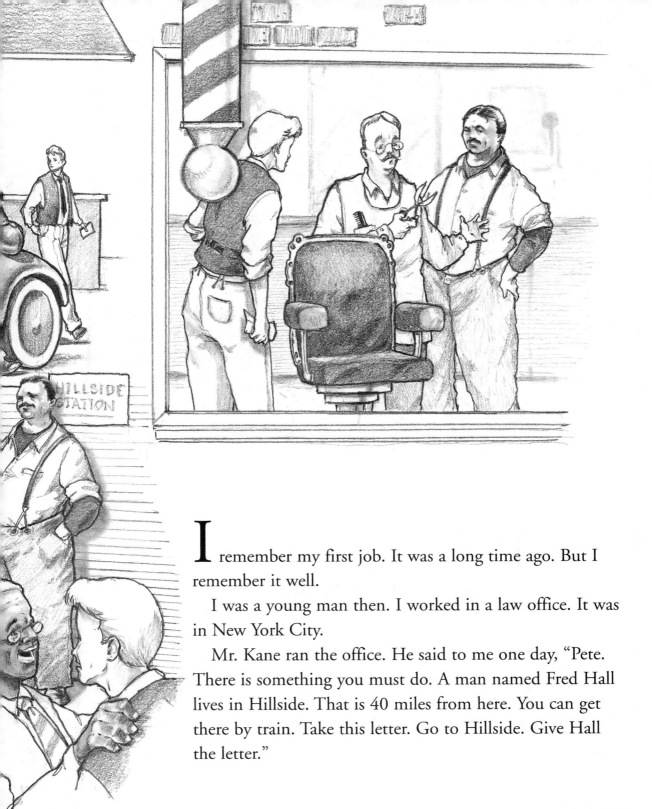

I remember my first job. It was a long time ago. But I remember it well.

I was a young man then. I worked in a law office. It was in New York City.

Mr. Kane ran the office. He said to me one day, "Pete. There is something you must do. A man named Fred Hall lives in Hillside. That is 40 miles from here. You can get there by train. Take this letter. Go to Hillside. Give Hall the letter."

Mr. Kane said, "Hall does not know you are coming. He does not want the letter. But he will *have* to take it from you. Give him this letter."

I put the letter in my pocket. Then I went to get the train.

I got on the train. Then I read the letter. It said that Hall had to come to New York. He had to come to our office. He had to answer some questions.

I got off the station at Hillside. I had heard that Hillside was small. But it was bigger than I thought.

I needed someone to drive me around. So I looked for a driver. I saw a man near the train station. He was standing next to a car.

I walked up to the man. I said, "I am looking for someone. His name is Fred Hall."

"Him? I saw him around here. That was a little while ago. He is a hard one to find. He is always running around. Always doing one thing or another."

The man smiled. Then the man said, "Sometimes he is doing no good."

I said, "That sounds like Fred Hall."

"Do you want to find him right away?"

"Yes," I said. "I want to take the train back to the city today."

"Well, I can drive you around. You can pay me by the hour. We will find Hall, all right. I know most of the places he goes."

"All right," I said.

The man pointed to the car. I opened the door and got in.

The man said, "We can start at Andy's Store. Hall sometimes hangs around there."

The man said, "I guess you want to get some money from Hall. He never pays anyone a cent. He **borrowed** some money from me. That was a long time ago. He did not give it back. Hall is not a bad fellow. But that is how he is with money."

The man looked over at me. "But do not worry," he said. "Together we will get him!"

I loved him for it! Alone it would be hard to find Hall. But now I had a helper. I said, "I work in a law office. I have a letter for Hall. I must give it to him. Hall does not want the letter. But he will have to take it! That is the law!"

"Well," said the man, "we will surprise Mr. Hall!"

"Yes we will, driver," I said.

He said, "People around here call me Bill."

"Right, Bill!" I said.

Soon we were at Andy's Store. We went in together.

"Hello, Andy," said Bill. "Have you seen Fred Hall? This is a friend of his. He comes from the city."

Bill pointed at me.

Andy looked at me. Then he looked back at Bill.

"Well," Andy said slowly, "Fred was in here before. But he left. I think he went to get his hair cut."

Bill said, "Thanks a lot. We will keep on looking."

We went to Jake's Barber Shop.

Bill asked right away, "Have you seen Fred Hall?"

"Who?" said Jake.

"Fred Hall," I said. "I am looking for him."

Bill said, "This is a friend of Fred Hall. He came all the way from the city."

Jake looked at me. Then he said, "Hall was here. But he left. That was five minutes ago."

"Come on," said Bill. "He must still be around here."

We went up and down the street. We went into every store. We nearly found Hall. But we always **arrived** just a few minutes too late.

Bill said, "Let us go to Main Street. Hall might be there. It has some shops that he likes."

So we went to Main Street. It was the same thing there. We came close to finding Hall. But we always just missed him.

"You know," said Bill, "Hall's mother has a farm. It is not far from town. Hall must have heard you were here. Hall must have gone there. He must be hiding on the farm."

We got into Bill's car.

Bill said, "I know Fred's mother. I once took her to the train. She had two big trunks. They were both very heavy. I hurt my back carrying them. Did she give me a tip? No, she did not! Let me do the talking."

We got to the farm. Bill knocked on the door. Hall's mother opened the door.

Bill said, "Remember me? I am Bill. I once took you to the train. This man is looking for your son. He has something to give him."

She said, "Fred is not here. I do not know where he is."

"Look here!" said Bill. "Enough is enough! This man came very far. He came all the way from the city. We know Fred is here!"

"No! He is not!" she said. "You can look all you want."

We looked all over the farm. We looked in the house. We looked in the barn. We walked around the fields. But Hall was not there.

It was getting late. I had to take the train back. I thanked Bill very much. Then I **paid** him for his time. I got on the train. I went back to the city.

The next day I saw Mr. Kane. He said, "Pete, did you see Hall? Did you give him the letter?"

"No," I said. "I looked everywhere. But I could not find him."

Mr. Kane was not happy about that. He said, "We must give Hall that letter! You must go back to Hillside. Go back with Dan Williams. Dan knows Fred Hall. Dan will help you find him."

Dan and I took the train to Hillside. We got off at the station. And there was Bill! He was there with his car. But I was very surprised. He was talking to Hall's mother! They were laughing and talking together!

I pointed to Bill. Then I told Dan, "There is a very fine man! He helped me a lot yesterday. He helped me look for Fred Hall.

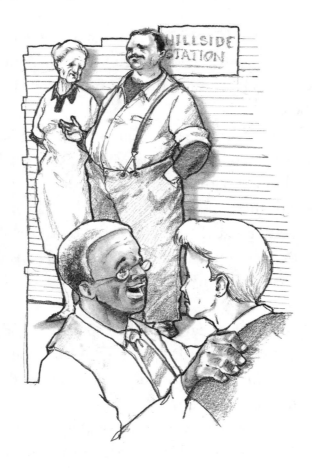

"Well," said Dan, "he should know Fred Hall. That is Fred Hall himself!"

I gave the letter to Fred Hall. He laughed loudly at me. Then he said, "Two of my neighbors heard about you. Can they meet you now? They are just about the only ones in town who did not see you when you were here."

Yes, I remember my first job. It was a long time ago. But I remember it very well.

TELL ABOUT THE STORY.

Put an X in the box next to the right answer. Each answer tells something (a *fact*) about the story.

1. Mr. Kane told Pete to
   - ☐ a. ask Fred Hall some questions.
   - ☐ b. bring Hall to the city.
   - ☐ c. give Hall a letter.

2. Andy said that he thought Hall went
   - ☐ a. to his house.
   - ☐ b. to Main Street.
   - ☐ c. to get his hair cut.

3. Mrs. Hall said that her son
   - ☐ a. had gone to New York.
   - ☐ b. was not on the farm.
   - ☐ c. was hiding some place.

4. Pete was surprised when he saw
   - ☐ a. Bill and Mrs. Hall talking and laughing.
   - ☐ b. how small Hillside was.
   - ☐ c. how friendly Jake was.

END EACH LINE.

Finish the lines below. Fill in each empty space with one of the words in the box. Each word can be found in the story. There are five words and four empty spaces. This means that one word in the box will not be used.

When you _____ a car, you must be ready for anything. The _____ ahead of you might suddenly slow down. Children _____ run into the road. You must _____ drive too fast to stop if these things should happen.

seen		car
	drive	
might		never

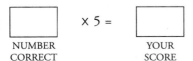

NUMBER CORRECT   × 5 =   YOUR SCORE

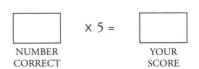

NUMBER CORRECT   × 5 =   YOUR SCORE

117

SHOW WHAT WORDS MEAN.

The words below are printed in **dark letters** in the story. You may look back at these vocabulary words before you answer the questions. Put an X in the box next to the right answer.

1. He said that Hall borrowed some money. The word *borrowed* means
   - ☐ a. did not need.
   - ☐ b. took for a while.
   - ☐ c. threw away.

2. They always arrived late. The word *arrived* means
   - ☐ a. came to a place.
   - ☐ b. looked around.
   - ☐ c. went home early.

3. He paid the man for driving him around town. The word *paid* means
   - ☐ a. gave money.
   - ☐ b. said hello.
   - ☐ c. liked very much.

4. Pete was in town yesterday. The word *yesterday* means
   - ☐ a. a week ago.
   - ☐ b. all the time.
   - ☐ c. the day before today.

☐ × 5 = ☐

NUMBER CORRECT   YOUR SCORE

THINK ABOUT THE STORY.

Here is how to answer these questions. First think about what happened in the story. Then work out the right answers. This is called *critical thinking*.

1. Which one is true?
   - ☐ a. The driver was Fred Hall.
   - ☐ b. Pete did not read the letter.
   - ☐ c. Hall was hiding on the farm.

2. It is fair to say that the people in Hillside
   - ☐ a. did not know Fred Hall.
   - ☐ b. liked city people.
   - ☐ c. helped Fred Hall.

3. The driver made believe that he
   - ☐ a. had never seen Fred Hall.
   - ☐ b. was looking for Hall.
   - ☐ c. was Mrs. Hall's son.

4. Pete should not have
   - ☐ a. gone to Hillside.
   - ☐ b. put the letter in his pocket.
   - ☐ c. believed the man who called himself Bill.

☐ × 5 = ☐

NUMBER CORRECT   YOUR SCORE

SPOT PARTS OF A STORY.

Stories have **characters,** a **plot,** and a **setting.** (See page 3.) Put an X in the box next to the right answer.

1. What happened last? (**Plot**)
   - ☐ a. Pete and Dan went to find Hall.
   - ☐ b. Bill said he would drive Pete around.
   - ☐ c. Mr. Kane gave Pete a letter.

2. Which best tells about Bill? (**Character**)
   - ☐ a. Everything he said was true.
   - ☐ b. Nobody liked him.
   - ☐ c. He was able to trick Pete.

3. Where does the story take place? (**Setting**)
   - ☐ a. in New Jersey
   - ☐ b. in Hillside
   - ☐ c. on a train

4. When did the story take place? (**Setting**)
   - ☐ a. weeks ago
   - ☐ b. a year ago
   - ☐ c. a long time ago

THINK SOME MORE ABOUT THE STORY.

Your teacher might want you to write your answers.
- What were some of the things Bill did to make Pete believe him?
- Why did Bill and Pete always "just miss" Fred Hall?
- Why do you think Pete remembered his first job so well?

Write your scores in the box below. Then write your scores on pages 120 and 121.

☐	**T**ELL ABOUT THE STORY
+	
☐	**E**ND EACH LINE
+	
☐	**S**HOW WHAT WORDS MEAN
+	
☐	**T**HINK ABOUT THE STORY
+	
☐	**S**POT PARTS OF A STORY
=	
☐	TOTAL SCORE: **Story 8**

☐ X 5 = ☐

NUMBER CORRECT   YOUR SCORE

119

Progress Chart

1. Write in your score for each exercise.
2. Write in your TOTAL SCORE.

	T	E	S	T	S	TOTAL SCORE
Story 1						
Story 2						
Story 3						
Story 4						
Story 5						
Story 6						
Story 7						
Story 8						

Progress Graph

1. Write your TOTAL SCORE in the box under the number for each story.
2. Put an X along the line above each box to show your TOTAL SCORE for that story.
3. Draw a line from X to X to see how much your scores go up.

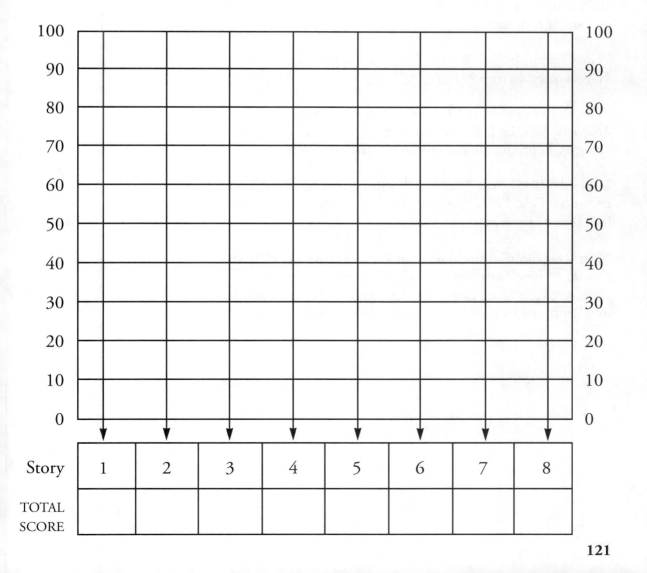

Story	1	2	3	4	5	6	7	8
TOTAL SCORE								

Acknowledgments

Acknowledgment is gratefully made to the following publishers, authors, and agents for permission to reprint these works. Every effort has been made to determine copyright owners. In the case of any omissions, the Publisher will be pleased to make suitable acknowledgments in future editions.

"The Game" from "The Safe" by Scott C. Mason Jr., *Scope,* March 1978 issue. Copyright © 1978 by Scholastic Inc. Reprinted by permission of Scholastic Inc.

"The Champ" by S. I. Kishor. Originally appeared in *American Magazine*, February 1941.

"The Old House" from "The Old Plantation" from *Tales for the Midnight Hour* by J. B. Stamper. Copyright © 1992 by J. B. Stamper. Reprinted by permission of Scholastic Inc.

"A Hard World" from "Brute's Christmas" by Dion Henderson, *Field & Stream*, Dec. 1951. Reprinted by permission of Larry Sternig & Jack Byrne Literary Agency.

"The Long Sleep" from "The Man Who Became a Fish" from *Famous Chinese Short Stories* by Lin Yutang. Copyright © 1948–1951, 1952 by (John Day Co.) Harper & Row Publishers, Inc. Reprinted by permission of Taiyi Lin Lai and Hsiang Ju Lin.